	DATE DUE		

Working Together Against
RACISM

People like Rigoberta Menchú, winner of the 1992 Nobel Peace Prize, are fighting to end racism and hatred. Ms. Menchú is fighting for the rights and equality of the indigenous people of her native Guatemala and other Latin American countries.

❖THE LIBRARY OF SOCIAL ACTIVISM❖

Working Together Against RACISM

By Rita Milios

THE ROSEN PUBLISHING GROUP, INC.
NEW YORK

It is impossible to tell whether a person is honest, friendly, intelligent, or rich based on skin color.

chapter 1

RACISM AND YOU

ANITA AND HER FRIENDS DROVE ALL OVER town looking for a restaurant. They finally decided on one none of them had tried before. They piled into the restaurant lobby. Another group came in right after Anita's, and the hostess seated them at the same time at tables right next to each other.

Anita and her friends were so busy talking that it took a while before they noticed that they hadn't received menus yet, while the group at the next table had already ordered and even had water. Finally, Anita's table received their menus, but it took a long time for the waiter to come over to take their order. By the time he did, the other table had already started eating their pizza!

"This is crazy," Anita fumed. "they are totally ignoring us."

"I think so, too," said her friend Brian. "I mean, I didn't want to say anything, but it's really weird."

Mercedes piped up with, "Why would they ignore us?"

"It's the same old story," Anita replied.

Everyone at the table looked at each other, then at the customers at the table next to them. The difference between the two groups was pretty obvious: Anita and her friends were all Latino; none of the kids at the next table were people of color.

The waiter had apparently decided that that table of kids deserved better service. By treating one group better than the other, he was behaving in a racist manner. Anita and her friends were experiencing discrimination because of racism. The waiter most likely feared or disliked Anita's group because he thought they were different from him. So he treated them differently. His racist attitude might have led him to think that all Latinos were poor, and could not afford to tip him. If the restaurant management also had a racist attitude, conscious or unconscious, the waiter might have felt he was pleasing the management by discouraging Latinos.

Racism is the mistaken belief that some groups are superior to others. This belief is justified by assigning one person's characteristics to an entire group.

A person who is racist cannot see beyond the color of another person's skin. He judges an entire group of people by the actions or stereotypes of one of its members. It is impossible, however, to tell whether a person is honest,

A common racist stereotype is that all Asians are excellent students.

friendly, intelligent, or rich by skin color. But such judgments are made all the time.

An example of this is: "John plays the piano. John is African American. Therefore all African Americans are musical."

This is faulty reasoning. John may be musical. John may be African American. But we cannot now extend this information to include all African American people. Let's compare this with:

"This is a rubber ball. It is soft. Therefore all rubber balls are soft." Since we know that there are hard rubber balls, we can see how this line of reasoning is wrong.

The system of apartheid in South Africa has been overthrown.

❖ THE INJUSTICE OF RACISM ❖

Racism is still a powerful force in the United States and around the world. In Annapolis, Maryland, in 1993, a group of African American Secret Service agents were treated badly by servers at a Denny's restaurant. This incident made the news. Many incidents just like it occur daily around the country and around the world.

Racism is manifested in many ways. Some 25 minority school children from a New York City public school were barred from an expensive toy store on Fifth Avenue. The teachers and some of

the students believed that the store manager assumed the children would be disruptive and more likely to shoplift because they were not white.

An African American student at Columbia University was asked to show his student ID card when entering the campus at night, whereas this never happened to his white friends. The guard held the racist assumption that young black men are more likely to be dangerous criminals than college students.

Racism is also acted out in more violent ways. In Florida in 1993, an African American tourist was dragged from his car and set on fire by several white men. In Wisconsin in 1989, a black teenager led an attack on another teen, beating him into a coma. The attacker was heard to say, "There goes a white guy. Get him." In California, in 1992, a Japanese businessman was stabbed to death in his home after he had been threatened with anti-Japanese remarks.

Racism exists all over the world. Racists come from all cultures. In South Africa, the former system of apartheid operated on the false basis that white people were superior to black Africans. Whites controlled society and kept blacks separate from whites by defining where they could live, what kinds of jobs they could hold, and what rights they had. The system of apartheid was challenged and fought against by

the black and other nonwhite South Africans. After years of struggle, some nonviolent and some highly violent, apartheid was outlawed, and the first national election for all South Africans was held. Much remains to be done to achieve equality of citizens in South Africa, but the work goes on. It is difficult to uproot such deep racism.

❖ WHY DOES RACISM DEVELOP? ❖

Racism has some highly unsavory relatives, among them prejudice and bigotry. The three usually keep company in a given individual.

Prejudice is prejudgment; we make up our minds about people before we know anything about them. Bigotry is the state of being obstinately set in one's own opinions and prejudices.

It is a rare human being who has no little trace of prejudice in his or her makeup. We are not born prejudiced, but the way of thought is so prevalent that we learn it almost before we learn to talk.

It is helpful to discuss these traits, try to identify them in ourselves, and weed out any we find. In that way we can come closer to a truly fair and just society.

❖ QUESTIONS TO ASK YOURSELF ❖

Racism affects everyone. Think about how it affects you. 1) Have you ever heard a racist joke? How did you react to it? 2) Have you ever been the butt of a racist joke? 3) What makes a person racist? 4) Do you think you are a racist?

chapter

2

ROOTS OF RACISM

WHY SHOULD THE COLOR OF PEOPLE'S SKIN matter? Skin color depends on the part of the world in which people's ancestors were born. It has nothing to do with their personal characteristics.

Looking at racism throughout history, it is evident that fear, anger, envy, and greed are all closely connected with it. Racists tend to have negative feelings about themselves or their own lives, so they blame their problems on others.

Having persuaded themselves that they are better than anyone else, racists can use that belief to justify seeking control over others.

Ignorance is also a factor in the development of racist ideas. Not knowing much about another group of people, it becomes easier to stereotype them; that is, to assume that they are all alike. For example, "All Asian Americans are good at math" is a stereotype.

The welfare system in the United States costs the country a great deal of money. Many prejudiced people, resenting this expense, tell themselves that most welfare recipients are African American. In fact, the numbers of white and black Americans on welfare are about equal.

❖ RACISM IN THE NEW WORLD ❖

The European colonists, opening up a new continent, wanted cheap labor to work the fields. Their greed for profit, along with their conviction of superiority over other races, brought about the institution of slavery in the colonies.

Africans of many different indigenous groups were kidnapped and enslaved. Shipped across the ocean in horrible conditions, the slaves were sold to the highest bidder and condemned to a life of hard labor.

The colonists thought of Africans as "savages," obviously less than human. Thus it followed that the slaves need not be treated as human beings. Most of them suffered inhumane living and working conditions, being beaten, flogged, and sometimes murdered.

The indigenous Americans were put in the same category. No thought was given to the fact that the Native American peoples had their own sophisticated cultures and religions. As the European settlements expanded to the west, Native American populations were forced from their ancestral lands. Some were taken as slaves, and countless numbers were killed.

Racism changed the history of Latin America and South America. Settlers came to Mexico from Spain in the 16th century and destroyed the indigenous cultures of the ruling Aztecs, who had built

up an advanced civilization and culture dating from the 12th century. The same was true in western South America, where the Native American Inca centered their empire in present-day Peru. The dominant culture was thereafter made up of light-skinned European settlers and their descendants.

In many parts of South America slavery was rampant. In Brazil, for example, about half of the population can trace their ancestry to West Africa. Brazil has the world's largest black population, after Nigeria. But racism also flourishes in Brazil. Brazilians of African descent generally have lower-paying jobs with less status, live in poorer communities, and face general discrimination.

❖ RACISM IN THE U.S. TODAY ❖

Slavery was abolished in the U.S. in 1864 at the end of the Civil War. Civil rights laws have been enacted that prohibit discrimination on the basis of race, ethnicity, religion, or sex. Many Native Americans live on reservations, lands reserved to them by treaties with the United States.

On the printed page it would appear that all was well with American minorities at the close of the 20th century. On the contrary, African Americans, Latinos, Asian Americans, Native Americans, Arab Americans, and other groups still suffer under racism.

The Vietnam War, among other things, contributed to some Americans' fear and hatred of Asians.

Latinos, or people of Latin America descent, are often victims of discrimination for speaking Spanish. In the 1980s and '90s efforts were made to declare English the official language of the U.S. This was based on the irrational fear that Spanish would replace English as the most commonly spoken language. It ignores several facts: that Spanish-speakers are a minority in this country; that most Spanish speakers are bilingual (that is, they speak both Spanish and English); and finally, that prohibiting the use of a native language violates a person's freedom. The "English-only" movement stems more from a fear and dislike of immigrants than from a real con-

cern for the preservation of the English language.

Asian Americans, a large and growing group, come from China, Japan, Korea, Thailand, India, Vietnam, and a number of other countries. The fact that the United States fought against Asian countries in World War II, the Korean War, and the Vietnam War has contributed to discrimination against Asians. The strong work ethic of Asian Americans and their determination to get ahead in their new land has given them growing economic strength. Consequently, they are often blamed for taking the jobs of people who were born in the U.S. At the same time, however, many Asian Americans find their national origin an obstacle to achieving success in the workplace.

The U.S. government has in effect various policies, grouped under the phrase affirmative action, that are designed to increase the proportion of African Americans, women, and other minorities in the workplace and schools long dominated by white men. In general, the policies require employers and institutions to set goals for hiring or admitting members of minorities.

The policies have always been controversial. Opponents have dubbed them "reverse discrimination" and blamed them for their own economic problems. Despite such objections, however, African Americans have not overcome the effects of past discrimination. Studies show

that they make half as much money as whites and have fewer opportunities open to them.

Religious groups can also be victims of discrimination and prejudice. For example, Jewish people have been persecuted throughout history. The Holocaust in Germany was a program of genocide. Genocide is the deliberate destruction of a racial, religious, or cultural group. Adolf Hitler, who led Germany from 1933 to 1945, was able to convince many Germans that Jews were responsible for Germany's economic difficulties. Hitler preached his mistaken idea of a pure, perfect society. Among those whom he wished to weed out were Jews, Gypsies, homosexuals, disabled people, and the mentally ill. Millions of people died as a result of Hitler's plan. Hatred of Jews, or anti-Semitism, is still a problem.

Organized groups that act on their racist beliefs and even model themselves on Hitler's Nazis still exist in the U.S. and other countries. Calling themselves neo-Nazis or using other descriptive names, they are white supremacists dedicated to undermining the ideal of racial equality. Some groups even advocate the complete separation of the races. Almost 350 such groups are documented in the United States today.

Assuming considerable prominence in recent years are the Skinheads, violent young supremacists who seek distinction by shaving their heads and wearing combat boots.

Adolf Hitler preached his mistaken ideas of a pure and perfect society to the people of Germany.

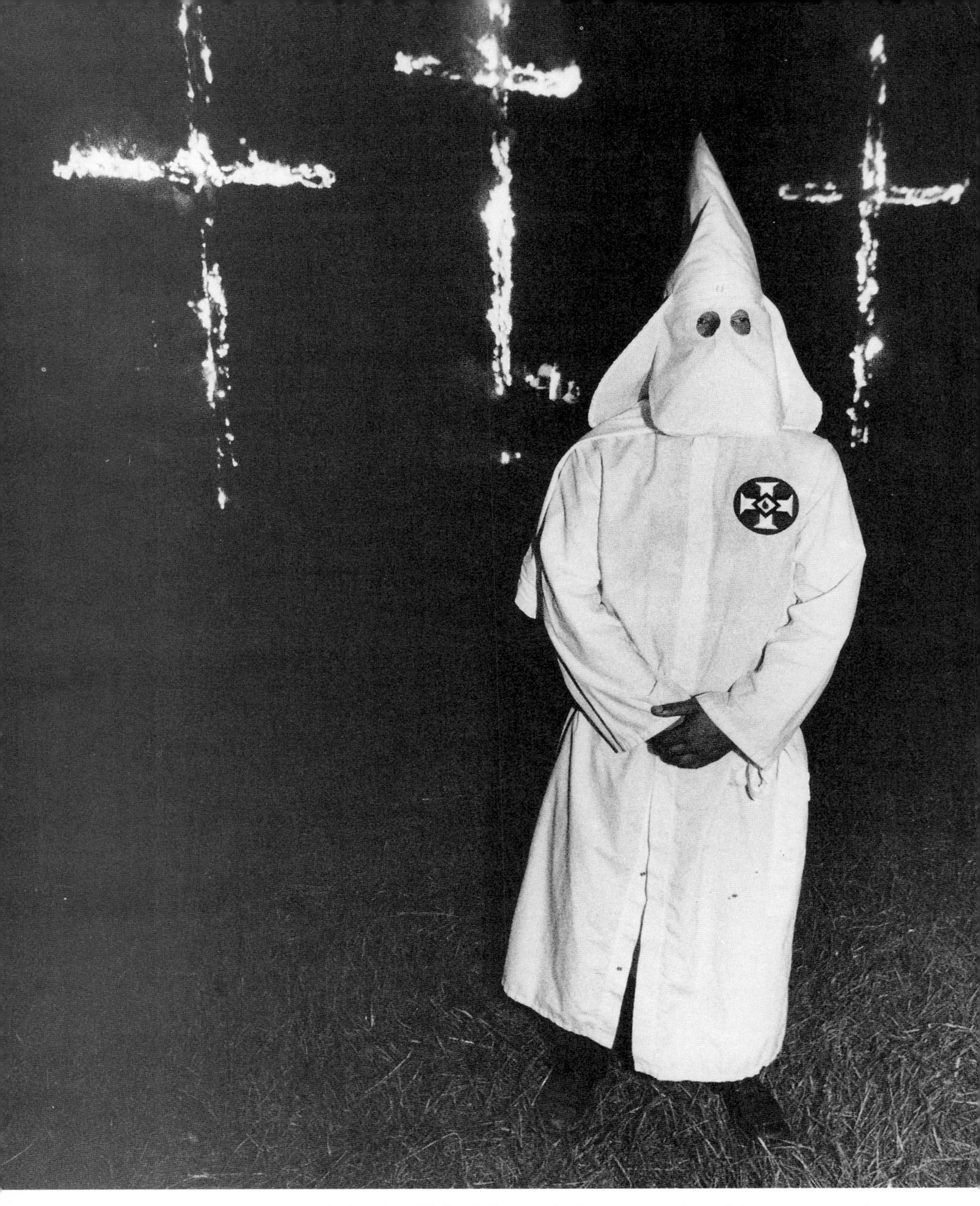

About 20,000 people in the United States belong to racist white supremacist groups like the Ku Klux Klan.

In July 1993, Skinheads were found to be involved in a bomb plot to destroy a church in Los Angeles and kill several prominent African Americans. Skinheads have been responsible for at least 22 deaths since 1990. They have attacked minorities, immigrants, homosexuals, and members of rival gangs.

The Ku Klux Klan, which was founded during the Reconstruction period after the Civil War, fell into obscurity but was never far from the surface. Periodically it rose again in widely scattered communities to spread its message of racial hatred with cross burnings and subtle methods of intimidation. Groups take many fanciful names, which sometimes makes it difficult to identify their early origins.

About 20,000 people in the United States are currently on record as belonging to white supremacist groups. But many more Americans than that are racist, whether or not they admit it even to themselves.

❖ RACISM IN THE PUBLIC EYE ❖

Racism can be seen in politics too. In the presidential campaign of 1988, then Vice President George Bush campaigned against Michael Dukakis, who was then the governor of Massachusetts. Bush tried to prove that Dukakis's program of releasing prison inmates on parole had resulted in terrible consequences. His campaign used the example of an African American man named Willie Horton who had been released under Dukakis's program and was later arrested for raping a white woman. Horton maintained, and still maintains today, that he is innocent. Bush successfully focused people's fears onto African American men, and in particular, the fear of their raping white women. In the South after the Civil War, this same fear was used by the Ku Klux Klan.

❖ OTHER FACTORS ❖

Advertising, movies, and the underlying attitudes of some talk show hosts stir up and reinforce feelings of prejudice and superiority. One example of the influence of advertising can be seen in many families of color, whose children want only dolls that have pale skin, blond hair, and blue eyes. They grow up feeling that because they don't match the dolls they are not worthy. The "Black is Beautiful" campaign has done much to improve this problem.

❖ QUESTIONS TO ASK YOURSELF ❖

Racism has existed throughout history. Let's take a look at some of our own feelings. 1) Does your school have students of various races? 2) Have you made friends of any teens of races other than your own? 3) Have you had the experience of being "put down" by someone of another race? 4) Have you noticed that some teens of minority groups exhibit racist tendencies themselves?

chapter 3

THE CIVIL RIGHTS MOVEMENT AND SOME OF ITS LEADERS

In the United States, racism has been exemplified by the inequality of treatment received by African Americans and other minority group members. Descendants of slaves are still fighting to secure full equality and recognition.

Despite the outlawing of slavery after the Civil War, it was not so simple to change the mindset of the whites, many of whom still considered blacks inferior, if not subhuman. Although legally free, African Americans did not enjoy full rights. Especially in the Southern states, laws required segregation of the races. Through appeals to fear and prejudice, Jim Crow legislation placed more and more restrictions on the blacks, until by the turn of the 20th century their status was almost as low as it had been at the end of the Civil War.

The clear call of the segregationists was "separate but equal." The doctrine was long used in support of segregation in the public schools and other public facilities. The U.S. Supreme Court

Jim Crow laws were supposed to keep blacks and whites "separate but equal," but there was nothing equal about those laws.

refused to rule it unconstitutional on the ground that such civil rights issues were reserved to the states. So blacks and whites ate in separate restaurants and attended separate churches, and their children went to separate schools. The "separate" was absolute, but the "equal" never approached realization. The African Americans' schools received inadequate funds. Their buildings were often old and badly maintained. Books and supplies were limited or nonexistent.

During these years forward-looking African Americans became active in efforts to improve the situation of their fellow blacks. The National Association for the Advancement of Colored People (NAACP), the oldest civil rights organization in the U.S., was founded in 1909. It fought many civil rights battles, perhaps the most notable of which was its victory in the landmark decision of the Supreme Court in *Brown* vs. *Board of Education*; the court declared the segregation of public schools unconstitutional.

That was a famous victory, but it did not win the war. Black children faced dangerous obstacles in attending schools formerly reserved for whites. In 1957 federal troops and state militia were called out in Little Rock, Arkansas, to prevent riots as the first black students entered a high school there. It took several more years before African Americans went to public schools as a matter of course.

Meanwhile, the civil rights movement was taking shape, and notable leaders were emerging.

Martin Luther King Jr., shown here with his wife, was awarded the Nobel Peace Prize in 1964.

❖ ROSA PARKS ❖

A black seamstress in Montgomery, Alabama, Rosa Parks was an early activist in her hometown's efforts to achieve equality. Her one seemingly small action helped to bring the civil rights movement into the national spotlight.

Under many Southern ordinances, African Americans were required to sit in the back seats of buses unless seats were vacant in the front. One day, Rosa took a seat in the middle of a bus. Shortly after, a white passenger got on and asked Rosa to give up her seat. Rosa refused, and she was arrested and sent to jail. Her action was not spontaneous, but planned to bring the bus segregation to public knowledge. When she was jailed, the civil rights leaders were ready for the next step. Two African American activists, Jo Ann Robinson and E. D. Nixon, moved to organize and unify the people against this injustice.

Jo Ann Robinson wrote a letter describing what had happened to Rosa. With the help of friends, she distributed copies of the letter to 35,000 black people in Montgomery. She asked that all black people refuse to ride the buses until the law that sent Rosa to jail was changed. This kind of protest is called a boycott. It is especially effective because it affects the economic interests of the community by refusing to buy the products of a company or companies, thus bringing social, political, and economic pressure for change.

The movement spread, with boycotts held throughout the South. Marches were organized, and nonviolent resistance was practiced. The people used only their physical presence to make their point. They sat in at segregated lunch counters. They did not fight back when police used firehoses and dogs to break up protest marches.

❖ MARTIN LUTHER KING, JR. ❖

This program of social action was largely organized by Martin Luther King, Jr., minister of a Montgomery church. He was a powerful speaker, and his sermons and other public addresses moved many people to activism. He founded the Montgomery Improvement Association to organize the bus boycott and traveled widely to raise funds for the civil rights effort.

King's activities won him the support of many Northerners, both black and white. In the early 1960s many of these supporters formed groups known as Freedom Riders, who rode trains, planes, and buses throughout the South calling for an end to segregation.

Dr. King's strategy of nonviolent resistance was a principle he had learned from Mohandas K. Gandhi, a great religious leader. Educated in England, Gandhi spent some years in South Africa and then returned to India to lead the Congress Party in the struggle to free that country

Rosa Parks and Jesse Jackson fought for **civil rights** in different but equally effective ways.

from British rule. Nonviolent action was an effective weapon in the struggle. Gandhi was assassinated in 1948, shortly after the success of the independence movement.

In 1963 King organized the March on Washington. To a gathering of some 200,000 he delivered the famous "I Have a Dream" speech, in which he said in part: "I have a dream that my four little children will one day live in a nation where they will not be judged by the color of their skin, but by the content of their characters."

Largely as a result of all these activities, President John F. Kennedy urged legislation to ban discrimination in government agencies and to enforce the desegregation of public facilities. Much of this legislation was enacted during the administration of President Lyndon B. Johnson, including the Voting Rights Act of 1965.

King himself was jailed several times. During one such episode, in Birmingham, he wrote "The Letter from Birmingham Jail," in which he spoke of his disappointment in the failure of white ministers to show more understanding of the plight of African Americans.

In 1964 King was awarded the Nobel Peace Prize. In 1968 in Memphis, Tennessee, he was preparing to lead a march of striking sanitation workers when he was assassinated by James Earl Ray.

Malcolm X was a leader of the civil rights movement until he was assassinated in 1965.

❖ MALCOLM X ❖

Malcolm X was born Malcolm Little, the son of a Baptist minister, in Omaha, Nebraska, in 1925. As a small child he was exposed to the nonviolent action theories of his father, who was killed when the boy was six. With this positive influence removed from his life, Malcolm turned to crime. At the age of 20 he was convicted of burglary.

In prison Malcolm read extensively, studying particularly the religious organization, the Black Muslims, and joined the faith. On his release, he went to Chicago and became a Muslim minister, taking the name Malcolm X. He became well known as a speaker and leader of the Black Muslims and a strong advocate of separatism for blacks. His views were at odds in some respects with those of the organization's leader, Elijah Muhammad, and in 1963 he split with the group and converted to orthodox Islam. Following a pilgrimage to the holy city of Mecca, he adopted the Arabic name El-Hajj Malik el-Shabazz. He then founded a lay group, the Organization of Afro-American Unity, which stressed black nationalism but was willing to work with whites toward common goals. In 1965 Malcolm X was assassinated while making a speech in New York. It was alleged, but never proved, that the killing was the work of the Black Muslims.

Nelson Mandela, South Africa's new President, has fought against the oppression of apartheid for most of his life.

❖ NELSON MANDELA ❖

In another part of the world, Nelson Mandela took a leading role in bringing equality to the blacks of the Union of South Africa.

For centuries the native black Africans had been subjugated by the whites, who had first come to the region in the 1600s. The subjugation culminated in the 1950s with adoption of the policy of apartheid, or complete separation of the races. Over the years, opposition to the policy strengthened, and numerous violent confrontations took place. In efforts to defuse the black resistance, self-governing Bantustans were established in the early 1960s, but the move merely intensified the resistance to apartheid.

Among the most prominent leaders of the opposition was Mandela, who joined the radical African National Congress (ANC) in the 1940s. In 1963 he was sentenced to life imprisonment for sabotage and conspiracy. From his prison cell Mandela continued to lead the ANC and the fight for equal rights for South African blacks.

In 1989 Frederik W. de Klerk was elected president of the republic, and gradually he implemented an easing of the repression of blacks. In 1990 he released Mandela from prison, and the ANC leader worked systematically for an end to apartheid. In the same years de Klerk ended the legal basis of segregation, and in June 1991 the race registration law was repealed.

On April 27, 1994, free elections were held to choose a multiracial assembly. Mandela was elected president of the Union of South Africa, with de Klerk as vice president. Thus, a lifetime of struggle brought ultimate victory to a great civil rights activist.

❖ DESMOND TUTU ❖

Operating from a religious perspective, Desmond Tutu has done much to further the defeat of apartheid in the Republic of South Africa. After education in Great Britain, Tutu served in posts in the Anglican church, and was appointed a bishop. He preached powerfully for peace between the races, urging nonviolent resistance and pointing out that whites could not be truly free until blacks were freed. Tutu traveled widely, carrying the message of equality of the races to churches in many countries. In 1984 he was awarded the Nobel Peace Prize. Later he was appointed Archbishop of Capetown.

❖ DALAI LAMA ❖

On still another continent, the fight for civil and religious rights goes on. In Asia, the ancient country of Tibet was seized by China in 1959, and its civil and religious leader, the Dalai Lama, was forced to flee into exile.

The religion of Tibet is Lamaism, a form of Buddhism. Its followers believe that the Dalai Lama (Dalai means "Grand") is the current reincarnation of the very first leader of Tibet. He was chosen as an infant and brought up with strict training to assume his governmental and religious role.

After the Chinese usurpation of his country, the Dalai Lama was received in India, where he was given land. He travels throughout the world, preaching the equality of all living beings. In 1989 the Dalai Lama was awarded the Nobel Peace Prize.

Archbishop Desmond Tutu preached for many years against apartheid and fully supported nonviolent resistance and peace between the races.

The Dalai Lama is forced to live in exile from his native Tibet.

❖ QUESTIONS TO ASK YOURSELF ❖

The struggle for freedom, equality, and civil rights continues all over the world, in movements large and small. Give some thought to the subject, and research some of the movements. 1) Who are some international civil rights leaders? 2) In what countries are struggles for equality still going on? 3) What are the issues surrounding these individual fights?

chapter 4

FACING TODAY'S CHALLENGES

HATE CRIMES ARE INCREASING IN THE UNITED States. A hate crime, or bias crime, is a crime committed because of the attacker's prejudice against the color, ethnicity, religion, gender, or sexual orientation of the victim. The rising tide of hate crimes is an indication of continuing racism in American society.

The riots in Los Angeles in 1992 provided shocking evidence of the hatred between people of different races. The spark that ignited the riots was the trial of four Los Angeles police officers for the brutal beating of Rodney King, an African American motorist who was stopped for speeding after a high-speed police chase. The beating was videotaped by a citizen living in an adjoining building. The trial and the tape were shown on national television. The result was acquittal of the officers by an all-white jury.

The riots in Los Angeles 1992 provided shocking evidence of hatred between people of different races.

Days of rioting and looting ensued. The death toll was put at 52, and damage was estimated at $1 billion. The verdict was widely attributed to racism.

The wave of hate crimes also struck New York City. In one incident in 1992, in Bronx County, an African American brother and sister, 14 and 12 years old, were attacked by four white teens who spray-painted them white, robbed them, and cut the girl's hair.

This crime reflected a trend in that both victims and attackers were young. The New York Police Department bias crimes unit reported that 60 percent of the crimes they investigated involved people under 20.

People of all races helped to clean up the aftermath of the Los Angeles riot.

❖ WHAT'S BEING DONE ❖

Racism is a growing problem among teens. As a teenager, you play an important role in stopping its spread. Your world is full of new challenges; it bears little resemblance to the one in which your parents grew up.

The United States has always been a multicultural society, but now the mix of cultures has become more diverse racially. The environment in which you live has the potential to be a celebration of human diversity and cultures.

Fighting racism takes time, effort, and dedication, but increasingly people are entering the battle. The efforts are especially notable in three areas: education, business, and politics.

❖ EDUCATION ❖

Multicultural education is becoming more popular throughout the country. Many colleges and universities now require students to take courses about other cultures. The focus is also changing in elementary and high schools. New textbooks contain more material on historical issues such as slavery and the treatment of Native Americans. Some schools have adopted an "Afrocentric" approach to education, giving students greater exposure to African and African American literature, history, and culture. Emphasis is also changing in areas where other minorities are strongly represented, especially Asian.

❖ BUSINESS ❖

Business large and small is coming to deal in a global marketplace, selling to and buying from countries around the world. Lack of understanding of cultural values of other races can cause serious harm to business. Many corporations now give workshops to employees on the cultural diversity of the regions with which they do business.

Labor unions and employee groups also have taken public stands against racism. For instance, the directors of the United Furniture Workers of America adopted a resolution opposing racism and organizations such as the Ku Klux Klan.

❖ POLITICS ❖

National and local elections are showing a sharp increase in the number of African American, Latino, and other members of minorities running for office and winning. In 1990, 300 U.S. cities had African American mayors. The campaigns of the African American clergyman and civil rights leader Jesse Jackson in the 1984 and 1988 Presidential primaries made history. Although he lost both races, he made a strong showing—in 1988 receiving 6.6 million votes.

For two centuries the United States Senate had been the stronghold of white males, with the exception of Margaret Chase Smith of Maine, who served from 1948 to 1972. In 1978 Nancy Kassebaum of Kansas was elected, and in 1992 six other women—one of whom was Carol Moseley-Brown of Illinois, an African American—joined her.

❖ QUESTIONS TO ASK YOURSELF ❖

Many schools are instituting multicultural programs to give students the opportunity to learn about different cultures. Let's see how this affects you. 1) What multicultural classes, activities, or events does your school offer? 2) What culture, other than your own, would you like to learn about? 3) Do you think multicultural programs such as these will help end racism?

chapter

5

ORGANIZING AGAINST RACISM

THE FIGHT AGAINST RACISM IN THE UNITED States is not over. Many new organizations have been founded in addition to the NAACP and CORE. Some have specialized goals, such as providing free legal advice or information and educational programs.

The following are some of those organizations and the issues they address. You can write to them directly for further information. Local communities often have organizations or branches of national groups. All of them would welcome volunteers.

Amnesty International
322 Eighth Avenue
New York, NY 10001

Amnesty International is concerned with human rights worldwide, focusing especially on

You and your friends can create your own group to fight against racism.

freeing political prisoners. It may use volunteers to join in letter-writing campaigns to foreign governments.

Anti-Defamation League of B'nai B'rith
823 United Nations Plaza
New York, NY 10017

The Anti-Defamation League works toward fair treatment of Jews and other minority peoples. The League publishes books and other materials designed to stop racism and prejudice through education. It also has training programs for teachers and students.

Asian American Legal Defense and Education Fund (AALDEF)
99 Hudson Street
New York, NY 10013

AALDEF provides legal services and education. The Fund publishes newsletters in Chinese, Japanese, Korean, and English. It operates a summer internship program for college students. Candidates may apply while still in high school.

Center for Democratic Renewal
PO Box 50469
Atlanta, GA 30302-0469

CDR promotes constructive, nonviolent responses to hate groups and racist violence. They publish reports which are used by journalists, professors, and policy-makers.

Congress of Racial Equality (CORE)
1457 Flatbush Avenue
Brooklyn, NY 11210

CORE works to achieve equality for all races. Its summer youth programs accept high school students as interns.

People must work together to end prejudice against all races. A peace march made up of over 25,000 people was held in Koreatown in Los Angeles. Koreatown was one of the main areas hit by looters and arsonists during the Los Angeles riot.

Hispanic Policy Development Project
1001 Connecticut Ave., Suite 310
Washington, D.C. 20036-5541

This group examines laws that affect Hispanic people and publishes the results. It works to improve the job situation and living conditions of Hispanics.

Indian Law Resource Center
60 E Street SE
Washington, DC 20003

The center is concerned with issues affecting Native Americans. It promotes their legal rights and works to stop discrimination against them.

National Association for the Advancement of Colored People (NAACP)
4805 Mt. Hope Dr.
Baltimore, MD 21215

The NAACP has a Youth and College Division which involves young people in the struggle for social justice. It offers anti-drug and teenage pregnancy workshops and SAT preparation clinics.

National Conference of Christians and Jews
71 Fifth Avenue, Suite 1100
New York, NY 10003

Among the youth activities of the NCCJ are weekend retreats called Anytown, whose goal is to build trust and understanding among students from different backgrounds. High school students form discussion groups and participate in various activities.

National Institute Against Prejudice and Violence
31 South Greene Street
Baltimore, MD 21201

This group works with schools, human rights organizations, law enforcement, and community organizations to respond to prejudice and violence.

Puerto Rican Legal Defense and
Education Fund
99 Hudson Street
New York, NY 10013-2815

PRLDEF works to combat problems Latinos face in obtaining education, health care, jobs, and housing. They also help Latino and other minority students enter the legal profession.

❖ **A DAY IN THE LIFE OF A VOLUNTEER** ❖

Andre works at Citizens for Peace and Equality. He found out about the group when they sent a speaker to his high school. He talked about dealing with racism in a multicultural environment. Andre's school is very mixed, and fights often break out between students.

"It's stupid," says Andre. "These kids are basically the same, but they think they can't get along."

Andre got CPE's phone number from a pamphlet the speaker, Keith, had given him. Andre called to volunteer. Keith was there and offered to work with Andre. Most of the people who worked there were volunteers. There were also a lawyer and a professor on call.

"We work from several different angles," Keith said. "Education, assistance, research, and networking. We send speakers into schools, businesses, or anywhere we're invited.

"Someone is here to answer the phones during the

day when people call to report racism or discrimination. We have an answering machine if someone calls after office hours. Whoever answers the phone listens and advises people on what do to, such as calling the police or contacting lawyers. Volunteers can't answer everything, though. Sometimes we have our lawyer or another expert call the person back." Keith then described the organization's other duties. Information gathering meant keeping track of race-related crimes and violence. CPE kept files of newspaper articles on many subjects. Networking meant keeping in contact with other groups, local, national and international.

"Andre, you would be great speaking to groups of young people. They often listen better to someone close to their age. They can be getting messages of racism from home, or from other youngsters. It's important to counter that with the strong message that racism is very bad."

The next week, Andre began his volunteering. One day a week after school Andre goes in to the office to get updated on things. He reads the newspaper files and talks to people in the office. He watches videos of famous speeches by civil rights leaders. Sometimes he quotes them. Every other week, Keith makes an appointment for Andre to speak at a school. He often speaks to kindergarten classes. First he explains what racism is. Then he answers questions.

One of Andre's favorite experiences was when he

Native Americans continue to fight against racism. These Cree Indians paddled 1,500 miles from Quebec, Canada to New York to call attention to their struggle to protect their lands.

led a lively discussion after an eighth grade class watched the film "Do the Right Thing."

"It's hard work," says Andre, "but I like it. It's really rewarding when I see that I'm making the kids think."

❖ QUESTIONS TO ASK YOURSELF ❖

There are many methods of fighting racism. These questions might help you decide where to start. 1) What goal is most important to you? 2) Which organization would you volunteer for?

chapter 6

WHAT YOU CAN DO ABOUT RACISM

People can use their creativity and enthusiasm to make a difference in their schools and communities. Many of them have devised highly innovative ways to demonstrate the evils of prejudice and racism.

A group of students in Sylvania, Ohio, formed a group called Promoting Ethnic and Cultural Equality, which they called by the acronym PEACE. They invited a nationally known speaker who uses the name John Gray for his deliberately provocative workshops. Gray's aim is to make his audience angry and thereafter make them think. He insults members of ethnic groups and goads them to reply. Most students are shocked when they learn that Gray is African American because he looks like a white man, a fact that enables him to see both sides of racism. "We are all racially prejudiced," he says. "Only by breaking the silence can we stop racism."

Another unusual approach to highlighting

racism was used by a a high school in Howell, Michigan, the hometown of a former KKK Grand Dragon. The school formed the Howell Diversity Club, designed to help stop racism and foster understanding among people of all races.

The diversity club created a game called The Game of Life. Players were given cards representing food, banking, education, employment, and jail. They were also given cards with coded symbols on them. These symbols—stars, colored dots, etc.—represented the race of each student, and what situations each would experience. Only the game keepers knew what each symbol meant. Depending on their symbols, some students were treated well when they went to rent an apartment. Others were told they were not welcome. Some students were denied food or were sent to jail. Although it was only a game, students felt the pain of rejection. Some students, successful in real life, faced failure for the first time. The Game of Life helped students step into someone else's shoes.

African American students in a high school in Winston-Salem, North Carolina, organized the Ebony Club to promote awareness and appreciation of the historic contributions of Africans and African Americans. The club hoped to demonstrate that having pride is one's race does not mean feeling superior.

Take the first step against racism by learning about it. Peace activist and decorated Vietnam veteran talks to a class in a Seattle high school.

Having stared very small, the Ebony Club now holds schoolwide assemblies.

All these groups and ideas came from students just like you. Take an active stand against racism. Start your own group. You can brainstorm ideas, invite a speaker, hold an assembly, or put up a bulletin board.

You can also contact organizations in your area to find out if they have any youth programs. If you aren't sure about the local organizations, contact the national headquarters. Often cities have task forces or committees on racism and discrimination. Contact them to see if you can attend one of their meetings. Take advantage of these resources, and use your own creativity as well. You can help to make a difference.

❖ QUESTIONS TO ASK YOURSELF ❖

The first step toward ending racism is to educate people. Let's think about how to do that. 1) What projects can you and your friends or your class develop to help educate others about the devastating effects of racism? 2) If you had to choose one aspect of racism to focus on, what would it be? 3) What other resources can you use to find out more about fighting racism?

Challenge those whose beliefs you question.

If we work together, we can end racism.

GLOSSARY

affirmative action Government policies designed to increase the proportion of African Americans, other minorities, and women in jobs and schools historically reserved to white men.

anti-Semitism Dislike or hatred of Jewish people.

apartheid Policy of racial segregation practiced in South Africa until 1994, when it was outlawed.

bigotry Intolerant devotion to one's own opinions or prejudices.

boycott Refusal by a group to have dealings with an organization, such as stores, eating places, or transportation companies.

discrimination The practice of making a distinction in treatment of others based on factors other than merit.

bias incident Criminal or violent act motivated by racism or prejudice.

hate crime Crime committed out of hatred of another race or culture.

prejudice Prejudgment of a person or group without knowledge of the facts.

racist Person who discriminates against or hates anyone or any group that is different from himself.

stereotype Generalization, often hurtful, used to describe all members of a group.

white supremacy The belief that people of the white race are superior to those of all other races.

ORGANIZATIONS TO CONTACT

Amnesty International
322 Eighth Ave.
New York, NY 10001

Anti-Defamation League of B'nai B'rith
823 United Nations Plaza
New York, NY 10017

Asian American Legal Defense and Education Fund (AALDEF)
99 Hudson Street
New York, NY 10013

Center for Democratic Renewal
PO Box 50469
Atlanta, GA 30302-0469

Congress of Racial Equality (CORE)
1457 Flatbush Ave.
Brooklyn, NY 11210

Hispanic Policy Development Project
1001 Connecticut Ave. NW, Suite 538
Washington, D.C. 20036

Indian Law Resource Center
601 E Street SE
Washington, D.C. 20003

National Association for the Advancement of Colored People (NAACP)
4805 Mt. Hope Dr.
Baltimore, MD 21215

The National Conference of Christians and Jews
71 Fifth Avenue, Suite 1100
New York, NY 10003

National Institute Against Prejudice and Violence
31 S. Greene St.
Baltimore, MD 21201

Puerto Rican Legal Defense and Education Fund
99 Hudson Street
New York, NY 10013-2815

1-800-347-HATE
National Hate Crime Hotline

FOR FURTHER READING

Dudley, William, ed. *Racism in America*. San Diego: Greenhaven Press, 1991.

Edwards, Gabrielle I. *Coping with Discrimination*, rev. ed. New York: Rosen Publishing Group, 1992.

Grunsell, Angela. *Let's Talk About Racism*. New York: Gloucester Press, 1991.

Kranz, Rachel. *Straight Talk About Prejudice*. New York: Facts on File, 1991.

Mizell, Linda. *Think About Racism*. New York: Walker & Co., 1992.

Osborn, Kevin. *Tolerance*, rev. ed. New York: Rosen Publishing Group, 1993.

Palmer, Ezra. *Everything You Need To Know About Discrimination*, rev. ed. New York: Rosen Publishing Group, 1993.

INDEX

ABOUT THE AUTHOR

Rita Milios is the author of over a dozen children's books as well as several adult books. Formerly an editor of a children's magazine, Ms. Milios taught writing at Toledo University's Continuing Education Department for seven years. Currently she teaches writing for a national correspondence school. In addition, Ms. Milios is an educational consultant, leading workshops for teachers and children.

Ms. Milios lives in Toledo, Ohio, with her husband and two school age children.

PHOTO CREDITS: AP/Wide World Photos
PHOTO RESEARCH: Vera Ahmadzadeh with Jennifer Croft
DESIGN: Kim Sonsky